66259

The UNITED STATES ENTERS *the* WORLD STAGE:
From the Alaska Purchase through World War I

1867–1919

The UNITED STATES ENTERS *the* WORLD STAGE:
From the Alaska Purchase through World War I

1867–1919

Christopher Collier
James Lincoln Collier

BENCHMARK BOOKS

MARSHALL CAVENDISH
NEW YORK

ACKNOWLEDGMENT: The authors wish to thank Thomas G. Paterson, Professor of History Emeritus, University of Connecticut, for his careful reading of the text of this volume in The Drama of American History series and his thoughtful and useful comments. The work has been much improved by Professor Paterson's notes. The authors are deeply in his debt, but, of course, assume full responsibility for the substance of the work, including any errors that may appear.

Photo research by James Lincoln Collier.
COVER PHOTO: *Corbis/Bettmann*
PICTURE CREDITS: The photographs in this book are used by permission and through the courtesy of:
Corbis/Bettmann: 12, 18, 20, 26 (top), 29, 32, 35 (top), 38, 40, 42, 45, 51, 52, 55 (bottom), 60, 83;
Joslyn Art Museum: 11; *Museum of the City of New York*: 26 (bottom); *National Archive*: 74 (bottom);
New York Public Library: 14, 16, 23 (top & bottom), 35 (bottom), 37, 48, 55 (top), 57, 59, 64 (top & bottom),
68, 70, 73, 74 (top), 77 (top & bottom), 80, 84.

Benchmark Books
Marshall Cavendish Corporation
99 White Plains Road
Tarrytown, New York 10591-9001

Library of Congress Cataloging-in-Publication Data

Collier, Christopher, (date)
The United States enters the world stage: from Alaska through World War I, 1867-1919
by Christopher Collier and James Lincoln Collier.
p. cm. – (The drama of American history)
Includes bibliographical references and index.
ISBN 0-7614-1053-8
1. United States—History—1865-1921—Juvenile literature. 2. United States—Territorial expansion—
Juvenile literature. 3. United States—Foreign relations—1865-1921—Juvenile literature.
[1. United States—History—1865-1921. 2. United States—Foreign relations—1865-1921.]
I. Collier, James Lincoln, (date) II. Title.

E661.C68 2000
973.8—dc21
                                                                          00-029483
Printed in the United States of America
3 5 6 4 2

CONTENTS

PREFACE

Over many years of both teaching and writing for students at all levels, from grammar school to graduate school, it has been borne in on us that many, if not most, American history textbooks suffer from trying to include everything of any moment in the history of the nation. Students become lost in a swamp of factual information, and as a consequence lose track of how those facts fit together and why they are significant and relevant to the world today.

In this series, our effort has been to strip the vast amount of available detail down to a central core. Our aim is to draw in bold strokes, providing enough information, but no more than is necessary, to bring out the basic themes of the American story, and what they mean to us now. We believe that it is surely more important for students to grasp the underlying concepts and ideas that emerge from the movement of history, than to memorize an array of facts and figures.

The difference between this series and many standard texts lies in what has been left out. We are convinced that students will better remember the important themes if they are not buried under a heap of names, dates, and places.

In this sense, our primary goal is what might be called citizenship education. We think it is critically important for America as a nation and Americans as individuals to understand the origins and workings of the public institutions that are central to American society. We have asked ourselves again and again what is most important for citizens of our democracy to know so they can most effectively make the system work for them and the nation. For this reason, we have focused on political and institutional history, leaving social and cultural history less well developed.

This series is divided into volumes that move chronologically through the American story. Each is built around a single topic, such as the Pilgrims, the Constitutional Convention, or immigration. Each volume has been written so that it can stand alone, for students who wish to research a given topic. As a consequence, in many cases material from previous volumes is repeated, usually in abbreviated form, to set the topic in its historical context. That is to say, students of the Constitutional Convention must be given some idea of relations with England, and why the Revolution was fought, even though the material was covered in detail in a previous volume. Readers should find that each volume tells an entire story that can be read with or without reference to other volumes.

Despite our belief that it is of the first importance to outline sharply basic concepts and generalizations, we have not neglected the great dramas of American history. The stories that will hold the attention of students are here, and we believe they will help the concepts they illustrate to stick in their minds. We think, for example, that knowing of Abraham Baldwin's brave and dramatic decision to vote with the small states at the Constitutional Convention will bring alive the Connecticut Compromise, out of which grew the American Senate.

Each of these volumes has been read by esteemed specialists in its particular topic; we have benefited from their comments.

CHAPTER I

The United States Looks Westward

The United States was, right from the beginning, a nation bent on expanding. The nation was barely a decade old when Thomas Jefferson made the famous Louisiana Purchase, buying what is today about a third of the country from France. In the 1840s the nation acquired the territory farther west, along the Pacific Coast. Americans very rapidly began to fill up all this land, hitherto thinly occupied by Indians. (The story of the displacement of the Indians is told in other volumes in this series.)

Yet despite this expansionist push, there has always been in America a lot of isolationist feeling. Protected on two sides by great oceans, and on two more sides by much weaker neighbors, a great many Americans, at times the majority, have felt that we should stay at home and keep out of the rest of the world's troubles. Yet in the years after the Civil War, when America was becoming one of the world's mightiest industrial powers, the United States was looking outward in a way it had never done before, not merely involving itself in troubles elsewhere but actually acquiring colonial possessions and greatly expanding foreign trade. That expansionist moment in American history is the subject of this book.

Jefferson's purchase of the huge piece of land that reached from New Orleans to the Rocky Mountains and the Canadian border turned American eyes westward. Although Indians had dwelt in the lands across the Mississippi for thousands of years, very few whites had seen the area. Small numbers of Spaniards and Mexicans lived in what is now the American Southwest and California; even smaller numbers of fur trappers and hunters wandered through the more northern areas and up into Canada. Americans really did not know what was out there—who the Indians were, what sort of animals and plants grew there. To find out, in 1804 Jefferson sent the celebrated Lewis and Clark Expedition into the Northwest, in part to explore the area, in part in hopes of finding a water route through to the Columbia River, which emptied into the Pacific and is now the boundary between Washington and Oregon. (The Lewis and Clark expedition is described in the volume in the Series called *The Jeffersonian Republicans*.)

This northwestern land, known as the Oregon Territory, was very fertile, and by 1841 Americans were beginning to settle there. By 1845 some five thousand Americans were living in the region south of the Columbia River. Americans were beginning to think of the land as theirs. Yet England had strong claims to it as well. Canada was British, and English and Canadian fur trappers and traders had long been exploiting the area, and had established a few trading posts there. The United States had been claiming land up to the 54°40' north latitude line, well into what is now Canada, but had also offered to compromise at the 49th parallel. The British, however, would not agree to this, for it would leave in American hands the Columbia River, the Strait of Juan de Fuca, and Puget Sound, all important shipping points.

The dispute was never very serious until American settlers began to pour in. By the 1840s, however, the settlers were asking the United States to set up a territorial government to provide laws, courts, and officials. A clamor went up in the United States for all the land up to the 54°40'

This famous painting shows American settlers moving through Indian territory in the area of the River Platte, in Nebraska, along a stretch of one of the overland trails into California and the Oregon Territory.

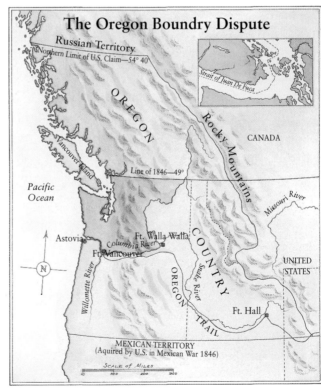

The Oregon Boundry Dispute

Russian Territory

Northern Limit of U.S. Claim—54° 40'

Strait of Juan De Fuca

OREGON

Rocky Mountains

CANADA

Line of 1846—49°

Pacific Ocean

Vancouver Island

Missouri River

Astovia

Ft. Walla Walla

Columbia River

Ft. Vancouver

COUNTRY

UNITED STATES

N

Willomette River

OREGON TRAIL

Snake River

Ft. Hall

MEXICAN TERRITORY
(Aquired by U.S. in Mexican War 1846)

SCALE OF MILES

A political cartoon shows America challenging England's John Bull to a fight over the Oregon boundary line. The caption says, "What, you young Yankee-noodle, strike your own father?"

line, with people shouting "Fifty-four forty or fight." As it happened, the president during this time was the expansion-minded James Polk. He decided to stand firm against England. The English, for their part, did not want to knuckle under, but the Oregon Territory was only a small part of the vast British Empire and the English government did not want to disturb its commercial ties to the United States over the matter. And in 1846 they offered to compromise. The line was drawn at the 49th parallel, continuing the existing Canadian-American borderline, with a loop going south around the bottom of Vancouver Island. The British could still bring ships into the Juan de Fuca Strait and the Columbia River. So the matter was settled. Oregon became a state in 1859, Washington in 1889, and Idaho a year later.

With the acquisition of the Oregon Territory, the United States now had an outpost on the Pacific. Then in 1848 at the treaty ending the war with Mexico, the United States got California, New Mexico, and Arizona. By chance, almost immediately gold was discovered in California. The gold hunters began to flood westward, along with an increased number of settlers headed for Oregon, and very quickly the Pacific lands were Americanized, with villages, towns, and cities springing up in what had been forests and plains. (The story of California is

1. Delaware	7 Dec. 1787	26. Michigan	26 Jan. 1837
2. Pennsylvania	12 Dec. 1787	27. Florida	3 Mar. 1845
3. New Jersey	18 Dec. 1787	28. Texas	29 Dec. 1845
4. Georgia	2 Jan. 1788	29. Iowa	28 Dec. 1846
5. Connecticut	9 Jan. 1788	30. Wisconsin	29 May 1848
6. Massachusetts	6 Feb. 1788	31. California	9 Sept. 1850
7. Maryland	28 Apr. 1788	32. Minnesota	11 May 1858
8. South Carolina	23 May 1788	33. Oregon	14 Feb. 1859
9. New Hampshire	21 June 1788	34. Kansas	29 Jan. 1861
10. Virginia	25 June 1788	35. West Virginia	20 June 1863
11. New York	26 July 1788	36. Nevada	31 Oct. 1864
12. North Carolina	21 Nov. 1789	37. Nebraska	1 Mar. 1867
13. Rhode Island	29 May 1790	38. Colorado	1 Aug. 1876
14. Vermont	4 Mar. 1791	39. North Dakota	2 Nov. 1889
15. Kentucky	1 June 1792	40. South Dakota	2 Nov. 1889
16. Tennessee	1 June 1796	41. Montana	8 Nov. 1889
17. Ohio	1 Mar. 1803	42. Washington	11 Nov. 1889
18. Louisiana	30 Apr. 1812	43. Idaho	3 July 1890
19. Indiana	11 Dec. 1816	44. Wyoming	10 July 1890
20. Mississippi	10 Dec. 1817	45. Utah	4 Jan. 1896
21. Illinois	3 Dec. 1818	46. Oklahoma	16 Nov. 1907
22. Alabama	14 Dec. 1819	47. New Mexico	6 Jan. 1912
23. Maine	15 Mar. 1820	48. Arizona	14 Feb. 1912
24. Missouri	10 Aug. 1821	49. Alaska	3 Jan. 1959
25. Arkansas	15 June 1836	50. Hawaii	29 Aug. 1959

told in the volume in this series called *Hispanic America, Texas, and the Mexican War*.)

This American takeover of the Pacific lands was perhaps inevitable. Neither the Spanish nor the British had done much about settling the area, whereas the United States had a rapidly growing population looking for places to spread into. American forays out into the Pacific Ocean

The treaty ending the war with Mexico brought the United States a huge chunk of land, including most of the Southwest and California. Here a scene from the Battle of Monterrey painted by a soldier who fought in it.

itself, however, and then beyond, were not inevitable, but part of the growing expansionist mood that was coming over the American people in the second half of the 1800s.

American interest in the Pacific had begun after the Revolution of the 1770s, when the country became free to do as it liked without interference from the British. In 1785 an American vessel, the *Empress of China*, sailed to China and returned with a profitable cargo. Other ships followed suit, mainly trading furs, much in demand by wealthy Chinese, in exchange for tea, silks, nankeen cloth, porcelain dishes, and more.

However, trading with China was not an easy matter. The Chinese considered Europeans rude barbarians, and wanted little to do with them. European traders were allowed into only a few coastal ports and could not travel inland to do business. The Japanese were even more determined to wall themselves off from European influence. For two hundred years they had kept contact with the West to a minimum. Shipwrecked European sailors might be held prisoners and were treated brutally.

But the Europeans were far ahead of the Asians in naval and military science and technology. In the late 1700s the British, through superior military might, forced open the Chinese port of Canton (now Guangzhou), and soon after took over the island of Hong Kong, making it a base for their Chinese trade. Other European nations established their own trading posts in China.

American trade with Asia was not crucially important, but Americans did not want to find themselves shut out of trade there. They began to insist on an *Open Door* policy in China, by which all Western nations would be allowed the same rights as the British had. The Chinese agreed: Why, after all, should they give the British a monopoly on trading rights? The British could object only if they were willing to go to war with the other nations, and gave way on the point. And by the second half of the 1800s a number of European nations had established trading posts at various places along the Chinese coast.

Japan remained closed, except for a tiny Dutch outpost on an island in the harbor of Nagasaki. But in 1853 the American president sent Admiral Matthew Perry to Japan with a small fleet, and over time Perry and events in Asia convinced the Japanese to open their doors to European traders bit by bit. The United States was now venturing out in the world in a larger way.

The United States had not yet acquired foreign possessions. It was soon to do so. Scattered through the vast Pacific Ocean are thousands of islands—some of them, like Hawaii, quite large; others so small that

The Chinese city of Canton was a major trading port for Europeans, who were only allowed to enter a strip of land along the waterfront. Here they built their warehouses and trading rooms, then called "factories." We can see the Canton factories with flags of European nations flying out front, including the American flag at center. Small Chinese ships, called junks, *carried goods out to the larger European ships anchored in the harbor.*

nobody lived on them. Many of these uninhabited islands were natural landing spots for birds. Inevitably these little islands became covered with what is called *guano*, or bird dung. In the 1800s guano was very valuable for fertilizer, and some Americans began importing it. To help them, in 1856 Congress declared that Americans could take possession of any uninhabited island not claimed by other nations. Several of these guano islands, like Midway, Baker's Island, Christmas Island, Howland's Island, and Jarvis Island, all located in the mid-Pacific, were thus claimed by guano importers for the United States.

A second island group that eventually fell into American hands, principally to keep it out of the grasp of other European trading rivals, was Samoa. One of the bigger of these islands, Tutuila, had a fine natural port at Pago Pago. Located in the mid-lower Pacific, the Samoan Islands were an excellent stopping-off place for ships coming around Cape Horn at the tip of South America, bound for Japan, China, and other Asian ports. Here ships could take on fresh water, vegetables, and, as steamships came in, load up with coal stores there.

In the 1880s Germany, England, and the United States fell into a squabble over the Samoan Islands. Eventually a deal was worked out by which rights were shared, and the islands ruled by the three nations jointly. In time, the United States got control of a group of these islands, now known as American Samoa; the rest are now independent. The American Samoan Islands today have complete local self-government but do not participate in the U.S. government the way states do.

Far more important than these island possessions was one much closer to home: Alaska. On clear days, Alaska is actually within eyeshot of Siberia, the western end of Russia. Russians began going out to Alaska to fish and trap furs in the 1700s, and by 1784 had a fort there. However, Russia made no attempt to settle the area: The Indians there, commonly called Eskimos, might be able to deal with the cold and fierce conditions, but it was not comfortable for Europeans. By the 1840s the Russians were looking around for somebody to buy Alaska: They realized that they could not defend the area; better to sell it before somebody took it away from them.

A few Americans saw the value of Alaska for its furs and fish, but to most it was a barren land of ice and snow. One of those who believed that Alaska had potential was William H. Seward, secretary of state under presidents Abraham Lincoln and Andrew Johnson. Seward was expansion-minded and was interested in Alaska. The Civil War held things up, but in March 1867 the Russians offered to sell Alaska to the United States. Seward quickly worked out a deal to buy the area for $7.2 million. There was a great deal of opposition: It seemed a huge amount of money to pay for a land that appeared to most Americans to be worthless. Some people said it ought to be called "Icebergia." Many agreed that the best name was "Seward's Folly." Nonetheless, Seward persuaded the Senate to agree to the deal in April, and six months later Alaska became an American possession.

It was known that there was gold in Alaska, and a series of gold discoveries in the 1880s and 1890s, especially in the famous Klondike field, brought a stampede of gold hunters, and Congress created a territorial government there. The area continued to develop slowly, and in 1959 Alaska became one of the United States.

Yet one more American possession that would go on to become a state was Hawaii. This group of islands was the closest stopping-off place to the American west coast. Right from the time Americans began trad-

This photo of Dawson, Alaska, in 1900 shows a rough frontier town that boomed as a result of the Klondike gold rush. In the sled are a moose and caribou shot for their meat and hides.

ing in the Pacific, their ships would usually put in at Hawaii. The islands had originally been settled by people of Polynesian descent, the same group of people who inhabited the hundreds of islands in the central Pacific. Over time, Americans and Europeans began to settle there, some of them missionaries determined to convert the natives to Christianity, more of them speculators setting up plantations in sugar and other crops. As had been the case with the American Indians, European diseases killed off huge numbers of the Hawaiians: Of the 200,000 original population, by 1890 only about 34,000 were left. In addition, American planters were bringing in large numbers of Chinese, Japanese, and other peoples to labor on the plantations. Foreigners soon outnumbered the originals, with whom they also interbred.

Over time this commercial activity bound Hawaii closer and closer to the United States, to the point where many Americans began to consider Hawaii an exclusive sphere of influence. Many Americans, however, were not ready to annex Hawaii as they had Alaska and the guano islands; nonetheless, they were certain that they did not want any European nations taking control there either. Although the original Hawaiians had their kings and queens who claimed to rule, in fact, by the post-Civil War period, well-to-do Americans, most of them born in Hawaii the children of planters, were actually in control of the legislature there.

The Hawaiians had mixed feelings about the situation: On one hand, they felt the were entitled to rule; on the other, they realized that they needed American strength against European nations, especially the Germans and English, who had their eyes on the islands. Over time various treaties were worked out, the most important being one that allowed Americans to use Pearl Harbor, near Honolulu, as a naval port.

Then in 1891 a new ruler, Queen Liluokalani, came to power. She was a strong, determined woman who resented American control of her domain. She made efforts to undermine the power of the Hawaiian-born Americans and Europeans who controlled the legislature and who con-

The Hawaiian Island of Oahu as it appeared to an American visitor in 1821. Even by that time American ships were stopping in Hawaii to trade for water, fresh fruit, vegetables, and meat.

spired against her through a secret organization. These people in turn revolted against the queen, and took over the island. They got American marines from a navy vessel anchored at Pearl Harbor to come in, and demanded that the U.S. government annex the islands.

But they had gone too far. Although President Benjamin Harrison approved annexation and sent a treaty to the Senate, the new president, Grover Cleveland, did not approve and withdrew the treaty. Nonetheless, the Hawaiian-born Americans who had taken over remained in power, and in 1893 declared Hawaii a republic. But they still wanted Hawaii to be annexed to the United States so they could avoid paying tariffs on their sugar, among other reasons. In 1898, when William McKinley had replaced Cleveland as president and many Americans had become expansionists during the war about Cuba, annexation was narrowly approved by Congress. And of course in time, like Alaska, Hawaii became an American state.

The question we must ask is this: Why did President McKinley approve of annexation while President Cleveland turned it down? The answer is that Americans were deeply divided on the whole question, not merely of annexing Hawaii but whether the United States ought to be acquiring colonial possessions at all. Let us see, then, what happened.

CHAPTER II

The Growing Call for Imperialism

Perhaps the most important movement in the world in the 1800s was the effort by "Westerners"—that is to say, Europeans and Americans—to colonize the rest of the globe. The process had started long before, as first the Portuguese and Spanish began to force their way into west Africa, the Caribbean, and South America, establishing colonies in such places as Mexico, Brazil, and Cuba. Soon the Dutch, French, and English joined the colonial movement, the English settling portions of North America, the French what is now Canada. Many of these nations acquired colonies in Asia as well. Europeans were able to take over such massive areas of the world because of their technical superiority: They had better and larger fleets, cannons, guns, and navigational equipment, in addition to well-established, sophisticated systems of commerce and finance.

In the late 1800s, newer nations, Germany and Italy in particular, entered into the colonizing game, hoping to establish empires to rival the British one. (The word imperialism refers to the control of one group of people over another—usually through the conquest of territory and setting up colonies.) Now Africa was being carved up, and as we have seen,

These two pictures suggest the force and extent of the European movement to colonize much of the world. Above, an early painting of the Spanish conquest of Mexico in the 1500s; at right, a British ship in the harbor of its colony of Hong Kong on the coast of China, which the British took three hundred years after the Spanish conquest of Mexico.

China, Japan, and other Asian nations were being forced open to Western trade.

In the years after the Civil War of 1861 to 1865, the United States was rapidly growing into a world power. A mighty industrial machine, based in rapidly growing cities, was overtaking even the great British manufacturing system. The nation was growing physically in size as pioneer farmers, gold hunters, adventurers, and settlers pushed into the vast western lands. Americans swelled with pride as they saw their country rapidly becoming one of the world powers. Indeed, might not America become first among the great nations of the world? To do so, the thinking went in the late 1800s, the United States must have colonies.

But it was not just national pride: Several new conditions, so it seemed to many, were forcing Americans to consider building a colonial empire. For one thing, there was a perception that the frontier was closed, or was at least closing. Up until even 1890, Americans had believed that if things went bad, you could always pull up stakes, go west, and start all over again on virgin land. This belief was given a push when Jefferson made the Louisiana Purchase in 1803, another push when the treaty with England in 1846 brought the Pacific Northwest into America, and yet another when the United States took over California and the Southwest after the war with Mexico. So by 1890 the western lands were filling up; towns were growing on the plains, in the fertile lands of the Northwest, along the California coast; and towns were turning into cities like San Francisco, Portland, Denver.

Actually the frontier was not nearly as "closed" as was often said: More grants for homesteads in the West were given after 1900 than in the years before. Nonetheless, Americans *perceived* that the frontier was closing, and the perception was what counted. This idea was taken up by one of the most influential historians America has ever had, Frederick Jackson Turner. He said that the experience of taking up land at the frontiers had made Americans self-reliant, democratic, and practical-minded.

Turner was afraid that without frontiers, Americans might be forced into a rigid class system in the European manner.

Making the situation more difficult was the rapid growth of the American population. Part of this population increase was "natural," that is, more Americans were being born than were dying. But a good deal of it was due to the huge wave of immigration, beginning in about 1870, that was roaring to a crescendo in the 1890s, precisely the moment when Americans were beginning to believe that the frontier was closing. (See the volumes in this series called *A Century of Immigration* and *The Rise of Cities*.)

Yet one more problem was the very might of the industrial system that was making Americans feel their oats. Inventors were constantly finding better, faster ways of producing things, both in factories and on farms. Consolidation of many small firms into huge combines, like U.S. Steel and Standard Oil, were making whole industries more efficient. The inrush of people from abroad and off the farms was providing a source of cheap labor. American farms and factories were churning out a supply of goods too large for Americans to consume. But they had to be sold somewhere. The answer, many felt, was to develop colonies where this glut of goods could be marketed.

Finally, many Americans were enduring hard times. There was a bad financial panic in 1873, and a worse one in 1893, which bankrupted thousands of businesses and threw millions of people out of work. Drought and terrible winters on the Great Plains in the mid-1880s had forced many farmers to sell their farms. The country seemed to be going through one crisis after the next; and once again the answer might be to sell goods abroad.

Americans, thus, had what seemed to many of them good reasons for looking outward. Influential writers were encouraging them to do so. One such was Josiah Strong, whose writings were widely read. Strong was an ardent Christian who believed that the rest of the world ought to

(above) By the 1890s, when this painting was made, Americans were no longer working mainly on farms, but in factories, like this steel mill. The workers are stopping for their noontime meal.

(right) Many Americans lived hard lives, as did these children, who instead of going to school, worked long hours in tenement workshops, as in this 1910 picture. The children are making artificial flowers, for which they would be paid tiny amounts of money, often earning only a few dollars a week.

be converted to Christianity. He also believed that Anglo-Saxons—meaning people of English and German descent—were particularly fitted to guide the world to a better way. The Anglo-Saxon, said Strong, was "divinely commissioned to be . . . his brother's keeper."

This attitude of superiority was not new, nor was it particularly an American one. All peoples tend to think that their ways are better than those of others, whether there is any evidence for it or not. Americans were no different from other people in this respect, and when they looked around at American industrial might and American success at making farms and building cities where there had once been field and forest, they saw evidence that they were a great nation. Senator Henry Cabot Lodge, a powerful politician, said, "From the Rio Grande to the Arctic Ocean there should be but one flag and one country." A newspaper editorialized, "A new consciousness seems to have come upon us. . . . The taste of Empire is in the mouths of the people." According to Josiah Strong, with the coming of steamships, the telephone, and the telegraph, the world was drawing "the peoples of the earth into ever closer relations." Americans really had no choice about it, Strong believed: They had to take the expansionist route.

An even more influential figure was Alfred Thayer Mahan. He was a naval officer who had thought hard about the problems caused by the closing of the frontier and the glut of goods Americans had produced. He believed that the solution was for the nation to find foreign markets for its goods. This in turn required a strong navy to protect American ships; it required colonies to serve as markets for American goods, provide raw materials like rubber and tin, and as places to store coal for steamships. After the Civil War, in order to save money, the American government had allowed the navy to deteriorate to the point where it was something of a joke. Through Mahan's influence, the United States began to build a modern steel-hulled, steam-driven fleet, which included powerful battleships.

A widely used term of the time was *manifest destiny*—that is, America had clearly been appointed by God to become a world power. Mahan said, "Whether they will or no, Americans must now begin to look outward." (For the roots of manifest destiny see the volume in this series called *Hispanic America, Texas, and the Mexican War.*)

But by no means were all Americans imbued with the spirit of manifest destiny. Millions of them considered the idea of building an American empire a serious mistake. This *anti-imperialist feeling* was based on several related ideas. (*Imperial* relates to the word "empire.") For one, there were those who believed that Americans would only get themselves in trouble if they involved themselves in the affairs of distant people. George Washington himself, in his celebrated Farewell Address, had strongly advised Americans not to get into what his secretary of state Thomas Jefferson later called "entangling alliances."

Further, many Americans believed that people untrained in democratic ideals and methods ought not to be made part of the American system, even as colonials. The Anglo-Saxon people were fitted for leadership, but, many Americans believed, other people would not really be capable of managing democracies.

Perhaps more important, a great many Americans insisted that the Declaration of Independence and the Constitution said all peoples had a right to govern themselves. A takeover of another country was, in effect, unconstitutional; certainly it was unethical and undemocratic. Many Americans, like people everywhere, had racist ideas; but it is also true that the United States is built on certain ideals, stated particularly in the Declaration of Independence, that all people are created equal and have a right to govern themselves. Indeed there has always been an idealistic streak in America. To many Americans, then, the very thought of building a colonial empire was wrong.

The movement against imperialism was led by a group called the Anti-Imperialist League. It said, among other things, that Americans

ought not to take over foreign peoples until "we have shown that we can protect the rights of the colored race of the South and the Indians of the West." The League was not large, but it included some of the most famous people of the day, among them Mark Twain, Andrew Carnegie, the philosopher William James, and the labor leader Samuel Gompers. Thus, when we think about the millions of Americans crying for the nation's manifest destiny, we must also remember that other millions were strongly opposed. The expansionists won the debate over Hawaii, but soon enough the battle between imperialists and anti-imperialists to control United States foreign policy would flare up again—and with deadly consequences.

CHAPTER III

The Spanish-American War

The Caribbean area has always been of intense interest to the Americans to the north. As far back as the 1600s American merchants and shippers were sending vessels to the Caribbean islands to trade American goods like pork, grain, and rum, for sugar, tobacco and, regrettably, black slaves. The Caribbean was an important trading zone for Americans.

Then, as the nation spread after the Revolution of 1776 to 1783, many of the Caribbean countries became neighbors: Cuba was only ninety miles from the tip of Florida; Mexico with its long Caribbean coast was on the American border. And all these places were inhabited largely by people of color whom most Americans thought were incapable of orderly self-government.

Beyond this, everybody had long realized that a passage across the narrow isthmus connecting North and South America would have immense value. To reach the Pacific trading posts in China, Japan, and Hawaii, ships from the important East Coast ports had to sail through the stormy dangerous strait at the tip of South America. In 1848 New Granada, which included what is now Colombia and Panama, made a deal allowing the United States passage across the isthmus in exchange for American protection from Europeans also interested in the passage. By chance, soon after the deal was made, the gold rush to California began. Thousands of eastern gold seekers took ships to the isthmus, crossed over by horse or on foot, and on the Pacific side took ships to San Francisco. The idea that a canal might be cut through the isthmus had long been in the air, and Americans were firmly of the opinion that any canal ought to be under their control.

Americans, thus, had come to think of the Caribbean as their sphere of influence, and did not welcome meddling by other nations there: As early as 1823 President James Monroe had announced the *Monroe Doctrine*, which said flatly that other nations must not seek new colonies in the Americas. The Monroe Doctrine had not initially been seen as important by European nations and even United States officials, but presidents and their secretaries of state had more and more come to insist on it. For example, in 1863 the French had sent troops to Mexico City and had set about conquering Mexico. After the Civil War, in 1865, Secretary of State Seward sent American troops to the Mexican border and demanded that the French leave, which they did. During the nineteenth century, American presidents had even thought about *annexing* (bringing under U.S. government control) certain Caribbean islands, like Santo Domingo and the Virgin Islands, but anti-imperialist feeling in Congress had been strong and these schemes had been turned down.

The Spanish, however, had been in the Caribbean, and Central and South America for centuries, and could not easily be asked to leave. In the 1820s a series of rebellions in various Latin American nations liberated many of their colonies, but the Spanish still clung to some of them. One of these was Cuba.

Cuba had long been a focus of American interest. At the beginning of the 1800s President John Quincy Adams had predicted that Cuba would one day become a state, and calls for annexation of Cuba came regularly.

Many Americans believed that Cuba, so close to the American shores, ought to be part of the United States. President John Quincy Adams predicted that it would happen.

For one thing, American businessmen had invested tens of millions of dollars in Cuban sugar plantations and other concerns. Over time, Cuba, like other Latin American countries, had attempted to free itself from Spain. A major rebellion broke out in 1868 that lasted ten years and though failing to gain independence from Spain, did bring an end to slavery in Cuba. Many Cubans had fled to the United States. They not only raised money to fight their rebellions against Spain but propagandized among Americans for their cause.

Through the decades leading into the 1890s, American sympathy for the Cuban rebels grew. America had, after all, fought its own colonial rebellion to gain its liberty. Nonetheless, there remained a good deal of opposition to getting involved in Cuban affairs. The anti-imperialists were against it on principle: It could lead to the building of an empire. Others felt that getting into the fight against Spain would be far more expensive than it was worth; and businesses with investments in Cuba did not want to see an upheaval there that would interfere with their profits.

Then in 1894 the United States government changed its policy toward taxation of imported sugar. The tariff on Cuban sugar was dramatically increased. The Cuban sugar industry, central to the island's economy, collapsed. A great many Cubans were thrown out of work and fell into poverty and hunger. Inevitably, the rebellious spirit flared up once again. In 1895 the Cuban patriot José Martí, in exile in the United States, landed a small army in Cuba, and marched toward the capital, Havana.

Martí was soon killed, but under other leaders the rebels had some success. However, the Spanish had 200,000 soldiers in Cuba, and went after the rebels in full force. Thousands of ordinary Cuban families were held behind fences in crowded, unsanitary camps. Fields were burned, villages destroyed. Diseases swept through the camps and the poorly fed civilians there died by the thousands.

By chance, in 1895, two New York newspapers, the *New York World* and the *New York Morning Journal* were fighting a circulation war. To draw in readers, they began headlining stories of atrocities committed against Cuban civilians. Further, they saw that a war would also build newspaper circulation and they urged Americans to get into the fight. The *World* and the *Journal* were not alone in creating "yellow journalism," (named for a comic strip character called "the Yellow Kid" appearing in one of the papers). Newspapers elsewhere indulged in the same kind of sensationalism. But the New York papers led the way, and were a major force in building a powerful popular demand that America join the war in Cuba.

Nonetheless, President Grover Cleveland resisted. He supported the position of businessmen who wanted to see a peaceful settlement between the Cubans and Spain on any terms; and, in any case, he tended to be anti-imperialistic. His successor, William McKinley, did not want war, but he wanted Spain out of Cuba. He even attempted to buy the island from Spain. In 1897, the Spanish government in Madrid, which did not want a war with the United States, offered the rebels a good deal of *autonomy* (self-government), provided that Cuba remain a Spanish possession. But the rebels refused: They wanted complete independence and at the moment were winning the war. For their part, Spanish officials in Cuba saw the deal as a sellout, and they too refused to accept it. How it might have ended nobody knows, but in February 1898, a rebel sympathizer working in the post office in Havana stole a letter written by the Spanish minister in Havana, which said that President McKinley was "weak and a bidder for the admiration of the crowd." The letter was published in the American yellow press, and increased public clamor by Americans to teach the Spanish a lesson.

But the uproar caused by this letter was nothing compared with what happened six days later. The American government had sent the U.S. battleship *Maine* into Havana harbor to impress the Spanish with the extent of American power. On the evening of February 15, 1898, the *Maine* exploded and sank, with the loss of 266 American sailors. The clamor in the press became a frenzy and the public demand for war became irresistible. In fact, nobody then (nor today) knows who was responsible for the explosion, but the press, on no evidence, blamed it on the Spanish. The Spanish, now desperate, began to give way on all points. McKinley still did not want a war, and there remained a good deal of anti-war feeling.

But the American mood was for a fight. In March, McKinley requested and Congress appropriated $50 million for the war. McKinley saw that there was no stopping the flood of public opinion. In April, he asked Congress to declare war. Congress did so; but it added the "Teller Amendment," insisted upon by the anti-imperialists, that after the war Cuba would belong to the Cubans, and would not be annexed by the United States. On the other hand, McKinley hoped that there would be some other way for the United States to control Cuba after the war. He did not think Americans' property would be safe under a Cuban government.

So the war was on. American volunteers poured in, and an unprepared peacetime army struggled to put together a fighting force. While it did so, the navy was already on the move. As a consequence, the Spanish-American War—which more accurately is sometimes called the Spanish-American-Filipino-Cuban War—began not in the Caribbean, but thousands of miles

The painting shows the USS Maine *exploding, as an artist envisioned it. Below is a photograph of the Maine after the explosion, showing it a total ruin.*

away in the Pacific Ocean, much to the surprise of the American public. How did this happen? A few months before, a youthful assistant secretary of the navy named Theodore Roosevelt had told Commodore George Dewey, commander of the American Fleet in the Pacific, that in case of war with Spain, he was to attack a Spanish Pacific possession, the Philippine Islands. When the declaration of war came, Dewey steamed into the Philippines, where he found a large Spanish fleet. The Spanish were no

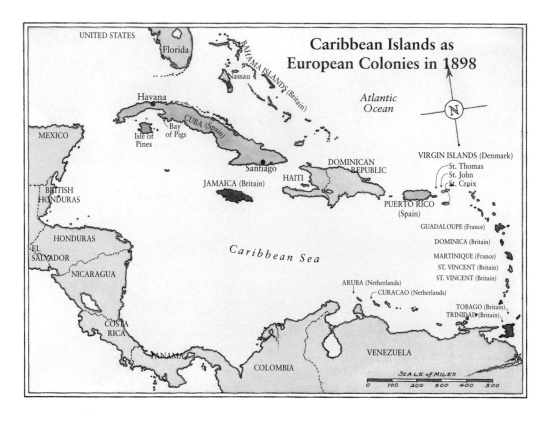

Caribbean Islands as European Colonies in 1898

match for the newly built American battleships, and the fleet was quickly destroyed. President McKinley, always cautious and thoughtful, momentarily delayed. Should he try to take over the Philippines?

Meanwhile, the army was getting itself organized, and by June had landed 17,000 troops in Cuba. At the same time, a fleet from Spain arrived at the harbor of Santiago de Cuba, where it lay at anchor, protected by shore batteries of cannons. U.S. troops marched on Santiago and there fought the only significant land action of the war. For a moment it was touch-and-go. The most memorable action of the war came when the same Theodore Roosevelt, now a colonel leading a volunteer group of cavalrymen known as the Rough Riders, made a charge up San Juan Hill above Santiago to victory. Roosevelt and his men acted with great bravery, and Roosevelt soon rode his fame into the presidency.

By this time an American fleet was blockading the Spanish fleet in Santiago harbor. On July 3 the Spanish admiral tried to make a run for it, but superior American firepower destroyed his fleet. The war was effectively over. Meanwhile, American troops invaded another Spanish possession, Puerto Rico. After nineteen days and three American deaths, the Spanish commander surrendered that island, too.

The Americans lost 5,462 dead, but most of these died of accident and disease, many of them in army camps in the United States; only 379 died on the battlefield. An exultant Secretary of State John Hay, in his office safe from death and disease, proclaimed it "a splendid little war." When the peace was finally signed the *New York Journal* ran a headline saying, "HOW DO YOU LIKE THE JOURNAL'S WAR?" It was not a high point in American journalism.

Two Spanish soldiers taken prisoner by Americans after the Battle of San Juan Hill.

POSSESSIONS ACQUIRED BY THE UNITED STATES 1856 TO 1917

Year	Accession	Area, sq. mi.
1856	Johnston Atoll (Johnston and Sand Islands)	0.5
1863	Swan Islands[1]	1
1867	Alaska	589,757
1898	Midway Islands	2
1898	Wake Island	3
1898	Hawaii	6,450
1898	Palmyra Atoll	4
1898	Philippines[2]	115,600
1898	Puerto Rico	3,435
1898	Guam	212
1899	American Samoa	76
1903	Panama Canal Zone[3]	553
1914	Corn Islands[4]	4
1916	Navassa Island	2
1917	U. S. Virgin Islands	133

[1]Turned over to Honduras in accordance with treaty signed 22 Nov. 1971.
[2]Ceded by Spain in 1898, the Philippines constituted a territorial possession of the U. S. until granted independence 4 July 1946.
[3]Under U. S. jurisdiction in accordance with treaty of 18 Nov. 1903 with the Republic of Panama. Returned to Panama in December 1999.
[4]Leased from the Republic of Nicaragua for 99 years but returned to Nicaragua 25 Apr. 1971.

Helping Cubans win their independence had been easy, partly because the Cubans themselves had done much of the dirty work and dying before American troops arrived. But there was still the matter of the Philippines, and that would prove not easy at all.

Few Americans knew anything about the Philippine Islands, even where they were located. The *archipelago* (a group of islands) consisted

The Spanish fleet made a run for it from the harbor at Santiago, but the Americans caught them and cut them down.

of more than seven thousand islands, most of them tiny. They had been controlled by Spain, especially Spanish Catholic missionaries, for centuries. The Spanish had treated Filipinos very harshly. The majority of them were plantation laborers held to their work, living lives of poverty and hard labor. Rebellion was constant, with one revolt after another blowing up and being put down time and time again.

Even though most Americans knew little about the Philippines, American merchants had been doing business in the islands for decades, bringing out sugar, coconuts, and hemp (used for making rope) in exchange for machinery, farm equipment, and tools. With a population of eight million ethnically mixed people, several times the population of Cuba, the Philippines were a significant market. Further, the islands made another good stopping-off point for American naval and merchant ships in the Pacific.

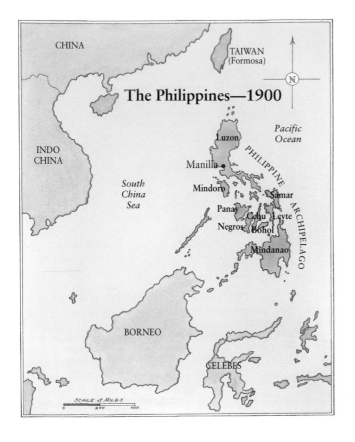

The Philippines—1900

CHINA

TAIWAN (Formosa)

INDO CHINA

Pacific Ocean

Luzon

Manila

South China Sea

Mindoro

Samar

Panay

Cebu Leyte

Negros Bohol

Mindanao

PHILIPPINE ARCHIPELAGO

BORNEO

CELEBES

SCALE of MILES

At the moment that the war started in Cuba, the Philippines were once again in the midst of a rebellion. The leader of the rebels, a tough, intelligent fighter named Emilio Aguinaldo, was in exile in Hong Kong. As we have seen, when the war broke out Commodore Dewey destroyed the Spanish Philippine fleet. The road to the capital city, Manila, was open, and Dewey urged Aguinaldo to take it. Aguinaldo returned to the Philippines, gathered his forces, and marched on Manila.

Back in Washington, President McKinley was in a quandary. He could not, of course, return the Philippines to Spain. McKinley did not want a European power moving in—the Germans were nosing around the area already. Americans, steamed up by the victory in Cuba and ideas of manifest destiny, were generally for annexing the Philippines. McKinley had an upcoming election to worry about, and in response to public pressure, sent troops to the Philippines. The Spanish very quickly surrendered Manila and the surrounding area to U.S. troops.

The situation now rapidly became very confused. Aguinaldo and the Philippine rebels had assumed that the Americans were there to help them throw off their Spanish overlords. The American officers in Manila were not sure what they were supposed to do, but very quickly the decision was made in Washington that Americans, not the rebels, would take

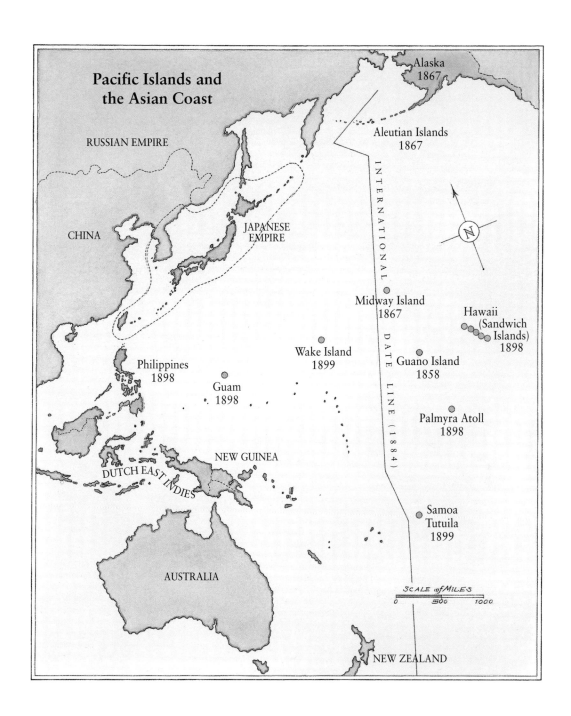

Pacific Islands and the Asian Coast

RUSSIAN EMPIRE

CHINA

JAPANESE EMPIRE

Alaska
1867

Aleutian Islands
1867

INTERNATIONAL DATE LINE (1884)

N

Midway Island
1867

Hawaii
(Sandwich
Islands)
1898

Wake Island
1899

Philippines
1898

Guano Island
1858

Guam
1898

Palmyra Atoll
1898

NEW GUINEA

DUTCH EAST INDIES

Samoa
Tutuila
1899

AUSTRALIA

SCALE of MILES
0   500   1000

NEW ZEALAND

control of the Philippines, at least for the moment. The principal concern remained that some other nation would take them over if the United States did not. For a short time the Americans and the Aguinaldo troops played cat-and-mouse. Soon it became clear to Aguinaldo that the Americans were simply not going to turn Manila over to him, and in February 1899 the two sides began fighting.

The American-Filipino War was one of the most vicious and dirty that Americans have ever fought. Both sides committed gross atrocities. Filipinos often buried American prisoners alive; Americans strangled Filipinos with ropes, or forced gallons of water down their throats. Fighting in thick jungles was exhausting for American troops, who were often hungry and soaked from rain and rivers. When Filipinos beheaded

The fighting in the Philippines was fierce and ugly. American troops of the 20th Kansas Volunteers cross a river, dragging their cannons after them on rafts.

Americans with their swordlike bolos, U.S. troops often retaliated by slaughtering a score of Filipinos, or burning a whole village.

The Americans had the advantage of firepower, but the Filipinos knew the territory and could fight a guerrilla war. It took 120,000 American troops three years to finally subdue the rebels. Aguinaldo was captured in March 1901, and by April 1902 the war was over. Over 4,000 American soldiers had died in it, along with 14,000 Filipino fighters, and at least 200,000 Filipino civilians. It was not a war Americans could be proud of.

The Teller Amendment, recall, promised not to keep Cuba after the war: But it said nothing about the Philippines. The decision to keep the Philippines committed the United States to a policy of imperialism—at least for the moment.

Concerning Cuba, the American government insisted that it hold certain controls over that country. These controls were outlined in 1901 in an amendment to a U.S. military appropriations

A cartoon showing the Philippine rebel leader Aguinaldo being crushed by American might. The American government had at first supported Aguinaldo in his attempts to rid the Philippines of the Spanish rulers.

bill that the Cuban government had to accept in order to be rid of the American army and navy. Called the Platt Amendment, it guaranteed American naval stations in Cuba, limited the new nation's authority to make treaties with foreign nations, forbade excess government debt, and authorized the United States to step in whenever it thought Cuban independence or law and order were threatened. This kind of a relationship is called a *protectorate*. The United States government established protectorates in several other Caribbean and Latin American nations in the first three decades of the twentieth century. Cubans hated this scheme because rather than guaranteeing their independence, it restricted it, but the United States had the power and forced the Cubans to accept it.

As a result of the American victory over Spain, the United States also took ownership of Puerto Rico. Relationships with Puerto Rico were mostly established by a series of Congressional acts and some Supreme Court cases, known to historians as the *Insular Cases*. (*Insular* relates to the word islands.) In effect these court decisions said certain parts of the American Bill of Rights did not necessarily apply to possessions unless Congress said so.

It is clear from all of this that Americans were very much of two minds about their new empire. The anti-imperialists still disliked the idea of an American empire in any form, and a great many other Americans had been sickened by stories that were beginning to come out about the atrocities committed by American troops in the Philippines. Nor were Americans willing to rule with as strong an arm as other imperial powers, particularly the Spanish. On the other hand, millions of Americans felt that the United States had fought for these possessions and protectorates, and had a right to run them in the nation's interest. Businesspeople in particular saw profit in them. From time to time the United States did send troops into Cuba (and, as we shall shortly see, other countries), frequently to protect American business interests.

But as time passed, Americans began to see the possessions and pro-

This cartoon shows the United States scooping up Cuba, Puerto Rico, and the Philippines, while the ghost of James Monroe wonders whether this application of the Monroe Doctrine is a good idea. The cartoon appeared in a very popular publication called Puck, *suggesting that anti-imperialist feeling was strong in the United States.*

tectorates as not only a moral problem but more trouble than they were worth. We cannot get too far ahead of our story here, but in the Jones Act of 1916 the United States promised the Filipinos their independence, which they got in 1946 after World War II. In the 1930s, a new American president would switch to a "Good Neighbor Policy," under which the United States would no longer interfere militarily in the affairs of Latin American nations.

Similarly, the United States gradually granted more self-government to Puerto Rico. In 1917 Puerto Ricans became American citizens, and in 1948 began electing their own governor. Ties with the mainland were strong, with tens of thousands of Puerto Ricans emigrating especially to

New York, or moving back and forth between both places. At the turn of the twenty-first century, Puerto Ricans were still divided about whether they wanted statehood, or to continue as a commonwealth; only a small portion demanded complete independence.

Compared with the great colonial empires of Spain, England, Holland, France, Germany, and others, the American one was small and brief, lasting in any real sense for about fifty years: Many Filipinos who fought the Americans in 1900 were still alive when independence became a reality in 1946.

Certainly the citizens of Hawaii, Alaska, Puerto Rico, Guam, and other American territories enjoy great advantages from their association with the United States. Though many of them resent the overbearing effects of American commerce and culture, U.S. armed forces protect them in time of war; our treaties with foreign nations bring economic benefits; and the United States provides a great deal of financial aid.

Nonetheless, many thoughtful Americans, right back to the days of the anti-imperialists in the 1890s, have felt that taking over other nations by force of arms did not square with the Constitution or American ideals of liberty and self-determination for all. Such people believe that the imperial push during this period was not the proudest moment in the history of America. The relationship of imperialism to democracy is surely a matter worth serious thought.

CHAPTER IV

Diplomatic Styles: Big Sticks, Dollars, and Morality

Nations have always battled over questions of power—who would be dominant over whom. However, in the 1890s, when the United States was in its imperialist mode, most of its forays into other nations were over commerce—that is, to give American businesses advantages in one way or another. The American push for possessions and protectorates at that time did of course involve military interests, as for example, setting up coaling stations in the Pacific; and a variety of patriotic and moral motives impelled the United States to fight in Cuba. But because large industrial and business corporations have a great deal of influence in government, commerce is always high on the list.

This was certainly true in the various American interventions around the Caribbean. To be sure, Americans wanted army and navy bases there, but mainly the idea was to open up this or that country to American trade, and make sure that Caribbean governments paid their bills to American and European bankers from whom they borrowed large sums of money. Of all American involvements in the Caribbean, certainly the most significant was the building of the Panama Canal. To

As early as the 1870s an expedition was sent from the United States to investigate a good route for a ship canal across the Isthmus of Panama. An artist on the journey made this lithograph of a Cuna Indian settlement near the Bay of San Blas, not far from where the canal would later be built.

put this story in perspective, we need to step back a little to get a good view of it.

Panama was for much of its history a part of Colombia. The Panama area, however, was divided from the rest of Colombia by mountains and swampy jungles: It was difficult to get by land and sea from one part to the other, difficult even to send messages. By the late 1880s Panamanians had long thought of themselves as a separate people. Indeed, during the 1800s there had been four serious rebellions by Panamanians against Colombia, as well as smaller uprisings. Panamanian independence had been a hot issue for a long time before plans for the canal were set in motion.

The idea of cutting a canal through the Isthmus of Panama was obvious, and had come up as early as the 1500s when the Spanish were first exploring the area. In the 1820s a group of American investors had considered digging such a canal, although they never did it. During the gold rush to California beginning in 1849, thousands of Americans crossed the isthmus to find ships on the Pacific side to carry them north to San Francisco, and in 1855-56, an American group built a railroad over the route. The idea of building a canal was more and more on people's minds.

Then, during the 1880s a French group, headed by the engineer who had built the Suez Canal in Egypt, attempted to dig a Panama Canal. The effort was defeated by heat, disease, and engineering problems. In 1889 they gave up, with the loss of millions of dollars and more than 20,000 lives.

But it was the Americans, facing on both the Atlantic and Pacific Oceans, who had the most to gain from a canal. It would save 8,000 miles on the trip around the bottom of South America from Eastern seaports to California. It would also substantially shorten the trip from the manufacturing cities of the East to Pacific trading ports in Hawaii, China, and elsewhere. As we have seen, the glut of American farm and factory products and the financial panics of 1873 and 1893, with millions unemployed, had made Americans acutely aware of the importance of overseas trade.

Beyond trade, there was the military. As we have also seen, the nation, at the urging of Captain—later Admiral—Alfred Mahan, was building a large, modern fleet. Such a fleet would have to operate in both the Atlantic and Pacific Oceans. A canal allowing easy passage from one ocean to the other would be of great value. For example, during the Spanish-American War it took one battleship in the Pacific seventy-one days to get to the fighting in Cuba. When the United States took over Hawaii and the Philippines after the war, the need for a canal became even more obvious. By 1900 a majority of Americans were firmly in favor of digging the canal.

There were two possible routes, one through Panama and the other through Nicaragua. The Nicaraguan route was much longer, but it ran at sea level and included a large lake for part of the distance. The Panama route had to pass over low mountains, and the area was rife with disease, but it was much shorter, and contained the partly completed remains of the French effort. It was a toss-up, really, and initially the U.S. government tended to favor the Nicaraguan route. But certain Wall Street bankers and politicians stood to gain handsomely if the Panama route was chosen. Through politicking and bribes, the Panama route was selected.

But of course, Panama still belonged to Colombia. The Colombian government wanted money for the rights to build the canal, and they wanted to have a good deal of control of it. By this time, William McKinley was no longer president. He had been assassinated in September 1901 by an anarchist. He was succeeded by the flamboyant Teddy Roosevelt, the hero of the charge up San Juan Hill during the fighting in Cuba. Where McKinley was cautious and deliberate—and occupied with the Cuban war—Roosevelt was bold and quick to seize opportunities.

Roosevelt knew that groups in Panama were ready to start yet another rebellion against Colombia. (Theodore Roosevelt should not be confused with his cousin, the later President Franklin Roosevelt.) In 1903 he quietly indicated that the United States would support the rebels. He sent some American navy ships loaded with marines steaming toward Panama. On the scheduled day a small handful of leading Panamanians simply walked into the local government offices and took charge. The Colombian admiral in Panama was bribed to steam away, and when Colombia sent in troops they were intercepted by a landing party of American marines. The Colombians really had little choice. It was all over in a few hours, with only one death reported. Teddy Roosevelt immediately recognized the rebels as the official government of the new nation of Panama, and within a few days a treaty was signed between the American and Panamanian governments allowing the United States to dig the canal.

A great many questions were raised about this treaty at the time, and continue to be raised. The treaty said that the new Panamanian government had "sovereignty" over the Canal Zone, a ten-mile strip across the country where the canal was to be dug. But it gave real power over the Canal Zone to the United States. American commanders there could do

Digging the canal was an immense engineering feat, requiring the removal of millions of tons of dirt and rock. Railroad lines were built just for this purpose.

Despite the heavy equipment used for the job, a lot of the work had to be done by hand. These men are digging holes for the dynamite used for blasting rock and dirt loose.

pretty much what they wanted, regardless of the wishes of the Panamanian government. Panamanians always resented the power that the United States possessed in their country.

President Roosevelt attempted to justify his actions by saying that the canal would be of immense value to people everywhere, which was certainly true. His attitude was that so important an accomplishment should not be held up by officials from small nations. But as he himself later said, "I took Panama." Historians today believe that other ways could have been found without trampling the rights of both Panama and Colombia, although to be fair to Roosevelt, many Panamanian and Colombian officials were not being simply patriotic but were hoping to enrich themselves out of the canal scheme.

Panama Canal

The Isthmus of Panama is fifty-one miles wide. The builders of the Panama Canal were aided by the fact that in hills above the seacoast there already was in place the twenty-four-mile-long Gatun Lake, as well as the smaller Miraflores Lake. The problem was that Gatun Lake was some eighty-five feet above the sea level entrance to the canal. To raise ships up to the lake, a series of *locks* was built—each 1,000 feet long, 110 feet wide, and 41 feet deep. A lock is a kind of boxlike channel with doors at each end, large enough to hold a big ship. The ship enters at the sea-level end, and the door closes behind it. Then the door at the other end is opened so that water from the lakes in the hills above can pour in. Gradually the water in the lock rises, lifting the ship. Thus, huge ships are raised up into Gatun Lake, and by reversing the procedure, dropped back down to sea level. The locks are built in side-by-side pairs so different ships can move in both directions at the same time. Ships are charged tolls for using the canal, which helps to cover the expense of running and maintaining it. It takes about eight hours for a ship to go through the canal, but because ships often have to wait their turn, the actual time is likely to be fifteen hours.

Today the canal is too narrow for the largest ships, like giant aircraft carriers and huge luxury liners. Further, with the development of missiles able to travel halfway around the world, the canal is less important to the United States military than it was in 1914. But its value for commercial shipping remains very great. Indeed, between 1915 and the year 2000, shipping increased from just a few tons to nearly 200 million tons a year.

Nonetheless, the deal was done, and the United States set about digging the canal. It was completed in 1914. The chief engineer for the job was Colonel George W. Goethals, and he did a superb job, though disease and accidents caused the deaths of 5,609 workers. Most of the original locks are still in place nearly a hundred years later, and the canal has never failed. No question about it, the Panama Canal has been of huge value to the maritime nations of the world, indeed to everybody who uses goods carried in ships. In 1977 a new treaty with Panama was negotiated, giving the Panamanians more rights in the Canal Zone, and on December 14, 1999, it was turned back to Panama.

By the early 1900s Americans had discovered that they could bully the small nations of the Caribbean into doing what they wanted. Europeans were content to let the United States police the Caribbean, as long as European interests weren't hurt.

Americans believed they had a right to take charge. The Caribbean had long been a sea of troubles. The small nations on the islands and the lands bordering the ocean had been part of various European colonial empires. By 1900 some had thrown off their masters, but had been unable to develop stable governments and sound economies. Many of the Caribbean people lived in near serfdom, while a small minority got rich on their backs. Americans believed that these small nations needed their help to keep their governments honest and their economies working. It is true that the American attitude was based largely on an Anglo-Saxon bias; it is also true that these Caribbean government officials were often profoundly corrupt, exploiting their citizens to feed their own greed.

In Teddy Roosevelt Americans had a president who agreed with them. He was a strong believer in using American power when necessary. His slogan was, "Speak softly, and carry a big stick," which is exactly what he had done to get the Panama Canal dug.

Once again American interest in the Caribbean largely revolved around commerce. Many of these nations were rich in minerals, oil, gold.

*(right) President
Teddy Roosevelt
was extremely
proud of his role
in seeing to it
that the canal
was dug. Here he
is sitting in the
engineer's seat of
one of the heavy
earth-moving
machines used
for digging the
canal.*

*(left) The first steamer
passes through the Pedro
Miguel Locks. The ship
was the SS Ancón.*

Most had fertile land where it was possible to make fortunes in crops like sugar, bananas, tobacco. European and American investors had long been drawn to the Caribbean, and owned many of the biggest plantations and rights to minerals and timber. Often government officials of these small nations were quite willing to let outside investors build large enterprises in their lands, so long as the officials were cut in on the profits. In many of these places officials expected to be paid off for permitting investors to come in. Of course, American investment brought economic development with many jobs and increased income for local workers.

As in Panama, rebellions in these countries were frequent. As everywhere, national pride played a part. In some cases the rebels were sincere in wanting to improve their countries; in other cases the "rebels" were other officials or army officers who wanted to collect the bribes themselves. A new government might cancel rights of a foreign company to cut timber or mine minerals, not only in order to collect payoffs from another company but also to end exploitation and get a better deal for the local residents. And, they might refuse to pay debts run up by the previous government.

In the past, American governments had not felt obliged to collect debts owed to Americans by foreign nations: That was the investors' risk. Roosevelt, however, decided to take on that responsibility. Further, he did not want strong European powers in the Caribbean, where they could threaten the Panama Canal. In a day before intercontinental missiles and air war, a battleship could attack the canal and destroy portions of it with cannon fire. Roosevelt was afraid that a strong European nation might occupy a Caribbean country near the canal entrance to collect some debts, and never leave. He now announced a rule, which became known as the *Roosevelt Corollary* to the Monroe Doctrine. This said that the United States had to have a police power in the Western Hemisphere: America, not some European nation, would step in when a Caribbean government showed "chronic wrongdoing or an impotence which results in a general loosening of the ties of civilized society."

American involvement in the affairs of Caribbean nations was complex, and lasted until a new policy was put into effect in the 1930s. One example is the case of Santo Domingo (now the Dominican Republic). This little island nation owed millions to American and European investors, but it could not pay, mainly because government officials were stealing most of the customs duties. Roosevelt in 1905 forced the Dominicans to let American naval officers come in to collect customs duties, giving 45 percent to the Dominican government and the rest to foreign investors. This scheme—which saw United States military occupation from 1916 to 1924—removed the debt and made the Dominican government solvent, but, inevitably, Dominicans resented American interference.

A similar situation arose in 1909 in Nicaragua. A rebellion broke out, and government forces executed two Americans who happened to get involved. The president was now William Howard Taft, who was trying to carry on

American power in the Caribbean is suggested by this picture of the president of Haiti surrounded by officers of the U.S. Marine Corps, who had a great deal to say about how the country was run.

Roosevelt's "big stick" policies. Taft supported the rebels and eventually arranged for American banks to control Nicaraguan finances. Nicaraguans were understandably resentful. When another rebellion broke out in 1912, Taft sent in troops; they stayed until 1933. And similarly, in several other places, financial and security arrangements like that with Cuba under the Platt Amendment were set up.

Taft termed his system *Dollar Diplomacy*, because his intent was to use the power of money instead of bullets. He believed Dollar Diplomacy was more humanitarian than using force. His main idea was to build up trade with Latin America and protect American investments there. Whether this policy benefited many North or Central Americans is open to question; but it certainly helped businessmen based in the United States.

The next president, Woodrow Wilson, took a different approach. He was determined not to recognize governments he thought had come to power illegitimately—that is by force or other unconstitutional means. He called this *Moral Diplomacy*. He first applied it to Mexico, where he quickly found it was harder to do in practice than in theory. In 1913 rebels took over a government that had worked well with the United

U. S. INTERVENTION IN THE CARIBBEAN, 1898–1934		
Place	Fiscal Control	Occupation
Cuba	1903–34	1898–1902, 1906–09, 1917–22
Panama Canal Zone	1903–99	1903–99
Nicaragua	1911–24	1909–10, 1912–25, 1926–33
Haiti	1916–41	1915–34
Dominican Republic	1905–41	1916–24
Honduras	—	1924–25

States. Wilson decided that the new leader was just another military dictator. In addition the new Mexican president planned a government takeover of American-owned oil wells. Wilson threw his weight behind other groups, who soon took over themselves. The new government was not able to control the nation, however, and soon local strongmen were ruling their own areas. One of these was the famous—or infamous, if you wish—Pancho Villa. He was not able to make himself Mexico's leader, but neither could the Mexican government capture him. In order to make

Some of the Mexican bandits under Villa who raided a New Mexican town, and were captured in the Mexican mountains, are under guard of American troops. Americans felt justified in sending troops into a foreign nation, but it was an unusual step.

Pancho Villa in a heroic pose on horseback.

himself a hero with Mexicans, he began attacking American citizens, even making raids on towns in Texas and New Mexico. President Wilson sent troops into Mexico to capture Villa, but the wily bandit always escaped, and lived until 1923, when he was assassinated. By that time the Mexican government had gained control of its nation. The net result of Wilson's Moral Diplomacy was yet more Latin American resentment of the powerful country to the north.

And this, in truth, was the real legacy of American involvement in the Caribbean: increasing hostility toward the United States. It is certainly true that all nations have a tendency to meddle in the affairs of their neighbors: in the twentieth century alone, nations like Russia, Germany, China, and Japan have conquered neighboring lands to rule as they saw fit. Even today many nations spend millions lobbying the United States Congress for aid and advantages.

And it is also true that American involvement in the Caribbean often brought some stability to this or that nation, although most of the benefit went to local and foreign businessmen, not to the bulk of the people doing the hard work.

But whatever the rights and wrongs of it, by the 1920s it was clear that the United States was harvesting a greater crop of resentment than was worth it. And in 1933, another President Roosevelt instituted his *Good Neighbor Policy*, under which the United States began to remove its military forces and stop meddling in Latin American affairs. (This story is told in the volume in this series called *The United States in World War II*.)

CHAPTER V

World War I

The Spanish-American War, and the events in the Caribbean we have been looking at, engaged the United States in the outside world in a way it had not been before. True, Americans had long been sending ships around the world to trade with people everywhere. Nonetheless, there had always been some feeling, as there still is, that the United States ought to keep its nose out of other people's affairs. But no matter what Americans *felt* about isolating themselves from the outside world, in fact they had always been involved, particularly through trade. The takeover of the Philippines, Hawaii, Puerto Rico, and the interventions in the Caribbean make this clear.

But if many Americans still believed that they ought to limit outside involvement, World War I showed them that they could not; and when it ended, the United States found itself a great world power.

World War I was one of those vast tragedies which even at the time many people thought could have been avoided. The events leading up to it are exceedingly complicated, and have been much debated. We need understand only a skeleton version here.

Europe for centuries has been a mosaic of entities, small and large, that were, and still are, constantly breaking up and re-forming. As with countries everywhere, among them there have always been intense rivalries, much warfare, and bloodshed. By the 1700s the two main rivals were England and France, who fought each other not merely in Europe but squabbled elsewhere over their growing colonial empires.

Then, in 1871, Germany was pulled together out of several smaller German-speaking principalities. This new nation was ambitious and set about building its own empire and challenging British and French dominance of Europe. In 1871 Germany fought a quick, but decisive, war against France. It took away the Alsace-Lorraine sector of France, which was home to a lot of ethnic Germans, and made France pay huge reparations—that is, goods and money to "repair" the war damages. The French grew bitter against the Germans.

The nations of Europe had always engaged themselves in networks of shifting alliances that were signed, abandoned, and re-formed in new ways. In general these agreements said that if country *A* is attacked, or attacked by this or that specific nation, country *B* will come to its aid. It will quickly be seen that if country *B* turns around and makes a deal with country *C* to come to its aid if attacked, that country *A* may find itself being drawn into a dispute that means nothing to it.

The rise of an increasingly strong Germany, with a powerful industrial machine and an expanding naval and military force, threatened France and England. Germans, in the 1800s, were producing some of the most important writers, composers, philosophers, and scientists of the day, and believed themselves possessed of a great culture. They felt themselves surrounded by enemies determined to keep them from their rightful place in the sun.

Inevitably, all these nations searched for allies, and by 1914 there existed two basic groups: the Triple Alliance, comprising England, France, and Russia; and the Triple Entente of Germany, Italy, and the Austro-Hungarian Empire. (This strange two-headed nation, combining

Verlag v. Herm. Beltz, Langensalza.

Gez. v. O. Handlow.

Germany did not really exist as a nation before 1870, but was a collection of principalities sharing a common language and culture. In the 1860s one of them, the militaristic Prussia, set about dominating the others, and welding them into one nation. Above, Prussians attack Hanoverians. With the nation unified, Germany then attacked France. The humiliating defeat left France and other nations worried about German might. At left, Germans preparing to attack the French at Metz.

RELATIVE STRENGTH OF PRINCIPAL BELLIGERENTS ON THE EVE OF WORLD WAR I

ALLIES	POPULATION IN MILLION	NATIONAL INCOME IN BILLIONS $	PER CAPITA INCOME $	RELATIVE SHARE OF WORLD INDUSTRIAL OUTPUT	IRON & STEEL PRODUCTION IN MILLIONS OF TONS	MILITARY & NAVAL PERSONNEL IN THOUSANDS	WARSHIP TONNAGE IN THOUSANDS OF TONS	TOTAL MOBILIZED FORCES IN MILLIONS
Britain	45	11	244	13.6	7.7	523	2,714	9.5
France	39	6	153	6.1	4.6	910	900	8.2
Italy	37	4	108	2.4	.93	345	498	5.6
Russia[1]	171	7	41	8.2	4.8	1,352	679	13.0
total	292	28	—	30.3	18.03	3,130	4,791	36.3[2]
United States	98	37	377	32.0	31.8	164	985	3.8[3]
CENTRAL POWERS								
Germany	65	12	184	14.8	17.6	891	1,305	13.25
Austria-Hungary	52	3	57	4.4	2.6	444	372	9.0
total	117	15	—	19.2	20.2	1,335	1,677	22.25[4]

This chart is intended to show the relative strengths of the major belligerent powers on the eve of World War I (1913–14). Note the overwhelming industrial strength of the Allies and the major addition to that when the United States entered the war on their side. Note also the very small army and navy of the United States before conscripting over four million men in 1917 and 1918.

[1]Left the war in 1917. Includes Poland, Finland, the Ukraine, Latvia, Lithuania, Estonia.
[2]An additional 2.6 million were contributed by Belgium, Rumania, Portugal, Greece, and Serbia.
[3]An "associated" power.
[4]An additional 2.85 million were contributed by Bulgaria and Turkey.

what are now roughly Austria and Hungary, was the remains of a once very powerful empire.) These two groups were poised against each other, and as early as 1911, people had begun to talk about an impending war. Nonetheless, as late as the spring of 1914, most sensible Europeans thought that war not only could be avoided but would be.

Then came the spark that lit the tinder. The Austro-Hungarian Empire had long had ambitions in its neighbor, Serbia, and had recently taken over two small regions that Serbia wanted. Serbs, in their turn, had always resented their bigger neighbor and had expansionist ambitions of their own. In June 1914 a Serbian assassinated the heir to the Austro-Hungarian Empire, Archduke Ferdinand. The Austro-Hungarian Empire sent an ultimatum, demanding that Serbia clamp down on certain nationalist and patriotic societies, and in other ways interfering in Serbia's affairs. It demanded much more than Serbians could possibly yield.

Now the web of alliances began to enmesh all of Europe. The Russians had always felt a friendship for their fellow Slavs. They decided to support Serbia against the Austro-Hungarians, and mobilized their army. The Germans, feeling trapped between a mobilized Russia in the east and France to the west, issued its own ultimatums to both France and Russia. Neither nation responded; both readied for war.

The Germans, fearful of having to fight the Russians and the French at the same time, decided to strike at France first, hoping to eliminate the western threat. Early in August Germany declared war on both nations and marched on France. Unhappily, the best route into France for the German armies was through neutral Belgium. The British, to this point, had no reason to come into the war; but they had an agreement to aid Belgium if it was attacked. So the British sent an ultimatum to Germany, and the European world came crashing down. The system of alliances that everybody had hoped would maintain the peace had brought about one of the most dreadful wars ever fought.

It must be said that some Europeans had been itching for a fight, and all the nations had built up huge military forces complete with new weapons like machine guns and poison gas. The French were still smarting from their defeat by the Germans in 1871. The Germans felt trapped between enemies; the French and English were worried that a rising Germany might come to dominate Europe; and the Austro-Hungarians were seeking dominance in the Balkans generally. Still, almost nobody wanted a war; and, if they had known what sort of a war it would be, they would have wanted it even less.

Americans were stunned by the outbreak of a major war, and as it became clear what a slaughter it would be, they were appalled. This was not going to be a "splendid little war." Americans were determined to stay out of it, and were grateful that they were separated from the conflict by the wide Atlantic Ocean.

Initially, most people thought that the war would be over in three or four months: A quick, decisive strike by one side or the other would end it. At first it appeared that the Germans were making that decisive strike. They swept through Belgium and into France, pushing down from the north toward Paris. They almost made it, but the French stopped them at the Marne River. By winter the two sides had settled down in parallel trenches running from the Swiss border to the English Channel, dividing Western Europe in half.

Now the sort of war it would be became clear. The American general Ulysses S. Grant had learned in the Civil War fifty years earlier that you had to have overwhelming numbers of troops to drive defenders out of well-made fortifications. The generals in World War I never seemed to learn this lesson. Incessantly, both sides threw troops against the other's trenches, only to have them slaughtered like hogs in a butchery by machine guns and cannon fire as they ran across the "no-man's-land" between the trenches. Sometimes the attackers would push the defenders back a few thousand yards, or a few miles; or even drive a wedge through the defenders' line. But most often the attacks failed, leaving thousands of dead and dying in the morass of mud, shell holes, and barbed wire in no-man's-land.

For the troops who did the fighting, the war was both physically and mentally demoralizing. There was always rain, and the trenches they lived in were thick with mud. Disease was everywhere; much of the time the men making those desperate charges were sick. Attacks were usually preceded by hours, or even days, of cannon bombardment. For the defenders it was torture. The unrelenting roar of the explosions and the

This German propaganda picture shows British soldiers surrendering to Germans. Trench warfare was even worse than depicted here. Soldiers were constantly wet and suffered continually from heavy bombardment. Most knew that they were unlikely to survive the next charge into no-man's-land.

concussive effects, along with the feeling that you might any moment be blown to pieces, drove men to tears, even to madness. The machine gun was even more devastating: a handful of machine-gun pits could stop an attack of hundreds of men, slaughtering most of them in the process.

The men knew in their hearts that they probably would not survive the war; would, most likely, not survive for more than a few weeks, or at best a few months. They would rise out of those trenches on the morning of an attack, hoping that they would somehow survive this one, but knowing in their hearts that they probably wouldn't; and that if they did manage to live they would die in the next attack, or the one after that.

And they did: 20,000 British soldiers were killed on the first day of the Battle of the Somme. On average, 5,600 soldiers were killed each day of the war. In all, 8.6 million soldiers, most of them young men, died in World War I. A whole generation of European men was wiped out, so that through the 1920s and 1930s, millions of children grew up without fathers, millions of women lived out their lives as widows, millions of older fathers and mothers lived into old age mourning sons.

World War I also saw the introduction of poison gas against troops. Indeed, it is the only war in which gas, since outlawed, was used significantly. Mustard gas in particular etched the lungs, causing soldiers to choke painfully to death. Troops were quickly issued gas masks, but they were not always effective.

The war was not fought in France only. Russians, Germans, Austrians, and Turks were also battling on the eastern front. Here, because of the vast open lands, there was less trench warfare. Germany and its allies, now called the Central Powers, advanced quickly into Russia. The Russians then drove them back. But in the end, the Germans were able to grind forward, slowly taking land to the east.

There was also fighting in Italy. During the Battle of Caporetto alone several hundred thousand Italians were killed, wounded, or captured by the Austrians. Eventually the Italians were able to regroup and drive the Austrians back. Other fighting went on in the colonies, particularly in Africa, where Germans, French, and English had possessions.

Most significantly for the United States, fighting also went on at sea. Initially it had been assumed that the great battleships of the various navies would blast away at each other. But the Germans knew that the British, long ruler of the seas, had the superior navy. The Germans developed fast, silent submarines—called U-boats—which proved very effective in sinking not only naval ships but supply and even passenger ships. In the end, submarines would prove critical to the war, for it would be attacks on American ships that would draw the United States in.

A cartoon published in a German magazine as the war was beginning shows the Kaiser in a military helmet in a car speeding toward Paris, with the goddess of Victory at his side. The wheels of the car have broken a British sword. Most people predicted a quick war, but victory proved to be very hard to achieve.

As stories of the holocaust on the battlefields appeared in American papers, Americans grew ever more determined to stay out. President Wilson issued proclamations of neutrality, urging Americans not to take sides. But inevitably they did. For one thing, there were eight million Americans of German descent who had always been proud of German culture and wanted to see a German victory. Irish-Americans, too, had for centuries been hostile to England, and wanted to see a British defeat, which they thought might help Ireland gain independence.

But American culture had been English at the beginning, and people of British descent dominated the nation. Americans read and loved English authors like Dickens and Shakespeare, and knew the legends of King Arthur and Robin Hood better than many American legends. They followed English fashions in dress and food. Americans had had their difficulties with the English dating back to colonial times. Nonetheless, many Americans, perhaps a majority, felt a kinship with the English, especially after the United States had joined in the great Anglo-Saxon imperialism of the late nineteenth century.

Americans also felt a certain affection for the French, who had aided the new nation during the Revolution, and whose culture Americans admired. Thus, the weight of American opinion favored the Allies against the Central Powers. Then, too, the British had better luck selling their position: Americans could read British books and magazines. More than that, the only working cable for transmitting news from Europe came through England. The British certainly exaggerated German cruelty in Belgium and elsewhere; but their propaganda against the "Huns" was widely believed. But whichever side Americans sympathized with, they were firmly for staying out of the war.

However, as the war in Europe settled down in the trenches, it became clear that both sides were daily using up extraordinary amounts of metal, gunpowder, clothing, food, and everything else needed to fight a war. The best source—indeed the only real source—for supplies was the United States. Buying these huge amounts of war supplies cost equally huge amounts of money. Once again, Americans would have to lend this money to the combatants.

Americans could have refused to sell goods or lend money for the war, and perhaps they should have, as it might have shortened the war. But they did not. Indeed, one secretary of state resigned because Wilson would not impose a ban on these activities. For one thing, there was a great deal of money to be made out of supplying the fighting nations. For another, American opinion now heavily favored the Allied side, and Americans were afraid that the British and French might lose the war if they were not supplied with munitions from American factories. And, of course, American bankers knew they could not collect debts if the Allies lost. In the end, the bulk of the war supplies were sold to the Allies, although certainly some went to Germany.

Inevitably, the Germans wished to stop shipments of munitions to England. In February 1915 they said that they would sink vessels sailing near the British Isles that might be carrying war matériel. Soon some Americans were drowned when ships were sunk. In May, a U-boat sank the British ship *Lusitania* with the loss of nearly 1,200 lives, 128 of them American. Citizens at home were in an uproar. Wilson, who was still trying to hold a neutral course, tried to calm tempers, and that fall tried to get the Allies and the Central Powers to begin peace negotiations.

They would not, and among Americans a feeling began to grow that the United States ought to build up its army and navy, just in case. Many Americans, including congressmen, government officials, and public figures, were determined to keep the United States out of the fight, and opposed this drive for "preparedness." Nonetheless, the bill to enlarge the military forces passed.

But Americans were still in no rush to join the war. In 1916 Woodrow Wilson ran for reelection on the slogan, "He Kept Us Out of War," and won, although by a tiny margin. Early in 1917 Wilson once again tried to get the Europeans to begin peace negotiations; once again the Europeans refused. Now the Germans decided to let their submarines loose, hoping to cut off all supplies going from the United States to England. They knew that England could not last long without American help and thought they could gain a quick victory. All vessels in the war zone would be sunk, the Germans declared. Wilson protested, and hoped that the Germans would not actually do it.

Just at this moment a note from the German foreign minister, Arthur Zimmermann, to the German minister in Mexico was revealed. The note said that if Mexico would attack the United States if it came into the war, Germany would see that Mexico got the American Southwest back—taken from Mexico in the war of 1846-48—when the Germans won. The celebrated Zimmermann note increased American hostility to Germany. Soon thereafter German submarines sank five American ships. The fat was now in the fire and on April 2, 1917, Wilson asked Congress to declare war on Germany. Americans were still not unanimously in favor of entering the war: Six senators and fifty representatives voted against going in. But the majority favored fighting.

From the Allied point of view, the timing could hardly have been better. A French offensive had just failed, with an enormous loss of life. French soldiers in many units, in despair that the war would ever end, or that they would survive it, were on the edge of mutiny. Great Britain was down to three weeks' supply of food, and its armies had been bled white. Germany was sinking over half a million tons of Allied shipping each month.

American soldiers in the trenches on the Piave front facing Austrians throw grenades in preparation for an attack. Enemy troops were close enough for hand-thrown grenades to reach them.

(left) Air war was in its infancy during World War I, but laid the base for the devastating air warfare of the next great war. Here an American fighting plane has set a German plane on fire; the German pilot is about to jump.

(right) A German aviator about to drop a bomb on Allied troops, some indication of how rudimentary air war was at the time.

Despite some modernization of the army and the arming of merchant fleets earlier, the United States could not be of much immediate help. While the navy was in good shape, the army was small and ill-equipped. Very quickly a draft was set up, which in time would draw 2.2 million young men into the army. Still, it took about eight months to train a soldier, who would also have to be equipped for combat. Wilson very quickly sent an already trained regular army division to France, but this was mostly to show American support.

More important for the moment was the American navy. The Americans convinced the British that transports had to sail in groups convoyed by destroyers and other small ships capable of warding off German submarines. These convoys did not eliminate ship losses altogether, but they reduced them substantially, and very quickly the supply situation for the Allies improved a great deal.

In the fall of 1917, as the Americans were still gearing up for the fight, a revolution swept Russia. What at first seemed to be democratic forces drove out the czar, and the Russians left the war. German troops who had been battling the Russians were now transported to France, and by the beginning of 1918 the Germans had the advantage of numbers. In the spring they decided on a major offensive, hoping to make a breakthrough before American troops arrived in large numbers.

At first the spring offensive succeeded, and by the end of May the Germans were once again at the Marne, fifty miles from Paris. But now American troops were arriving in force. In the crisis, the U.S. 2nd Division and some other units were thrown into the battle. On June 3 and 4, the Americans were rushed into a place called Château-Thierry. Here, fighting alongside some French troops, they fought the Germans for ninety-six hours, finally driving them back from the Marne. The next day the 2nd Division counterattacked into Belleau Wood. For three weeks they fought, pushing the Germans out of the woods and back three miles.

Then, at the end of September, the Americans joined in a great attack on the Germans at Meuse-Argonne—that is, where the Meuse River ran through the Argonne Forest. The initial attack was a huge success: 33,000 German prisoners were taken in one day. But the Germans proved to be tough and the Americans had a hard fight to drive them out of the forest. This was the last major campaign of the war and the only one in which Americans made up the bulk of the forces. But it was costly: Of 1.2 million American soldiers involved, 120,000—one out of ten—were killed or wounded.

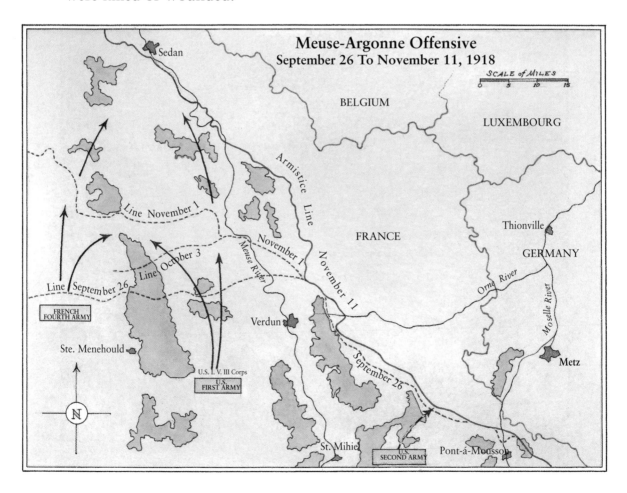

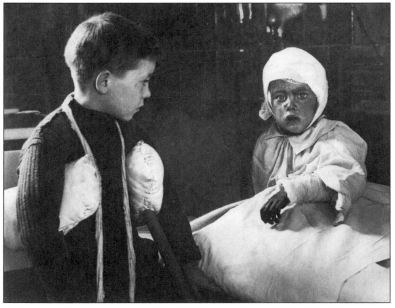

(above) The war left huge portions of France and elsewhere ravaged. This area outside of Poelkapelle, Belgium, shows typical devastation in December, a month after the war ended.

(left) It was not only fields and buildings that were damaged. These two British children were hurt during an air raid on London.

European National Boundaries, 1914

Europe After WWI

Atlantic Ocean

North Sea

Baltic Sea

NORWAY SWEDEN

FINLAND

ESTONIA

LATVIA

LITHUANIA

RUSSIA

DENMARK

EAST PRUSSIA

POLAND

EIRE

ENGLAND

London

NETHERLANDS

Brussels

Berlin

Warsaw

GERMANY

Paris

Prague

CZECHOSLOVAKIA

Vienna

Budapest

FRANCE

AUSTRIA

HUNGARY

ROMANIA

Bucharest

Black Sea

SWITZERLAND

YUGOSLAVIA

Belgrade

Sarajevo

BULGARIA

Sofia

PORTUGAL

SPAIN

ITALY

CORSICA

Rome

SARDINIA

ALBANIA

GREECE

TURKEY

Athens

SICILY

CRETE

Mediterranean Sea

SCALE of MILES

0   250   500

European National Boundaries, 1919

American soldiers of the 23rd Infantry Division firing 37-mm guns during the big advance in 1918 that ended the war. American's contribution to the war was small, but it was decisive. Note the extent to which the forest has been blown to bits.

At the same time, the British launched an attack at another part of the line, and they, too, pushed the Germans back. The German high command finally realized that they had been beaten. Kaiser Wilhelm resigned and the new German government sought an armistice. American involvement in the ground war had been relatively modest and it had been brief; but it had also been crucial, for it had provided just enough weight to tip

Influenza

Today we think of "the flu" as a relatively mild disease everybody suffers from occasionally that can be treated with drugs. In 1918, influenza, in certain forms, was a deadly and highly contagious disease and none of those drugs existed. There had been epidemics of influenza at least since the 1600s, but the one that struck in 1918 was one of the worst. It was particularly likely to strike younger people between the ages of twenty and forty. It swept through army camps, where millions of young men were living in close quarters. From September to November 1918, the major wave struck the United States, affecting 28 percent of the population, and killing 450,000 people, far more than were killed during the fighting. In fact, many more American soldiers died of the flu than from bullets—worldwide, the 1918 flu epidemic probably killed 15 million people.

the scales in favor of the Allies. In all, over 4 million Americans had been enlisted, nearly 50,000 of whom died in battle.

With the war over, President Wilson was determined that there would never be another such tragedy. In his principled way, he hoped to find ways for nations to work peaceably together. In January 1918, while the war was being hotly fought, he had offered a program of *fourteen points* he thought might be the basis for a negotiated peace. He now brought these Fourteen Points to the peace conference at Versailles, near Paris. Americans were seen as heroes in England, France, and Italy, and Wilson's prestige was high. Wilson was sure he could get his Fourteen Points through.

The Fourteen Points came down to four basic ideas: dealings between nations must thenceforward be open, with no secret agreements; arms would be limited and other measures taken to prevent future wars; each ethnic group would have "self-determination," that is, would decide for itself whether to form its own nation or join with another one; there would be an international organization to settle disputes before they turned into wars. This organization was eventually called the League of Nations.

Wilson was high-minded, but a lot of the other people at the conference were not. The French wanted to see the Germans seriously weakened so they could never again become a threat to France. Both French and English wanted reparations. And various victorious nations had secret agreements about carving up Germany's overseas empire. Wilson recognized that the war was not solely the fault of the Germans, and he fought hard to get a reasonable settlement. But the animosity of the Allies toward Germany was running strong. The League of Nations went through; but the Germans were required to give up some territory to France, and pay what would be enormous reparations. The peace conference also bundled together several Balkan groups to make up Yugoslavia, in hopes that the Balkans would live peacefully together and not trigger another great conflict. Similarly, Czechoslovakia was formed out of Czech and Slovak minorities in the Austro-Hungarian Empire. The Germans, inevitably, balked at the terms, but the French threatened to march into Germany, and the Germans had to give in.

Wilson went home not entirely satisfied, but he believed that the League of Nations could correct errors and injustices later on. He was reckoning, however, without his enemies at home. The leader of these was the Republican Senator Henry Cabot Lodge of Massachusetts, who hated the Democrat Woodrow Wilson, and had misgivings about the League. Other people shared these misgivings, feeling that the United States was giving away too much of its power to an international body. Lodge cleverly orchestrated the debate over the treaty to go on for weeks, while opposition to it among the public developed. Many objections

Senator Henry Cabot Lodge, who hated Wilson, fought to prevent the United States from joining the League of Nations.

were raised. Wilson was willing to compromise on some points, but not on the League.

Still, American support for the League in some form was strong. In September 1919 Wilson set off on a lengthy speaking tour to persuade Americans to back the League. (There was, of course, little radio and no television then.) At the end of six weeks he was exhausted and told by his doctors to go home. Soon he had a stroke which left him helpless for weeks. Wilson never fully recovered and became more stubborn than ever. He refused to compromise. In the end the Senate voted against the League. The peace treaty, without American participation in the League, was signed in 1921, but by then Wilson had left office.

History is full of might-have-beens. Historians have speculated that if the Germans had been given easier terms, they would not have felt the need for a strong man to redeem them, and we would never have had Adolph Hitler and World War II. And perhaps if Wilson had been willing to compromise more on the League and the Fourteen Points, the United States might have joined and possibly helped to ward off the war

A cartoon shows Wilson grasping at straws as he drowns in a pool of public opinion against his League of Nations plan.

to come. But we can only speculate. The United States did not join the League of Nations, and World War II did come.

With the rejection of the League of Nations, Americans again tried to insulate themselves from European politics. Over the next two decades the United States confined its overseas activities to keeping control of its Latin American neighbors and managing its interests in the Pacific, especially the Philippines. High American and European tariffs of the 1930s further attempted to isolate the United States from foreign entanglements (a story told in the volume in this series called *The United States in World War II*). Thus the American adventure with imperialism and European wars ended in disillusionment and withdrawal. But by 1940 it was clear that Americans, despite the desires of many, could no longer stand in the wings of the global stage. The bombs dropped at Pearl Harbor in Hawaii in December 1941 ended any hope of avoiding a major role in world affairs.

BIBLIOGRAPHY

For Teachers

Beisner, Robert L. *From the Old Diplomacy to the New, 1865-1900.* Wheeling, IL: Harlan Davidson, 1986.

———. *Twelve Against Empire: The Anti-Imperialists, 1989-1900.* Chicago: University of Chicago Press, 1985.

Brands, H.W. *T.R.: The Last Romantic.* New York: Basic Books, 1997.

Chambers, John Whiteclay. *To Raise an Army: The Draft Comes to Modern America.* New York: Free Press, 1987.

Cohen, Warren I. *America's Response to China: A History of Sino-American Relations.* New York: Columbia University Press, 1990.

Crosby, Alfred W. *America's Forgotten Pandemic: The Influenza of 1918.* New York: Cambridge University Press, 1989.

Ferrell, Robert H. *Woodrow Wilson and World War I.* New York: Harper and Row, 1985.

Gilderhus, Mark T. *The Second Century.* New York: Scholarly Resources, 2000.

Hagan, Kenneth J. *The People's Navy.* New York: The Free Press, 1991.

Hunt, Michael. *Ideology and U.S. Foreign Policy*. New Haven: Yale University Press, 1987.

Keegan, John. *The First World War*. London: Hutchinson, 1998.

Kennedy, Paul. *The Rise and Fall of the Great Powers*. New York: Random House, 1987.

Le Feber, Walter. *The American Search for Opportunity, 1865-1913*. New York: Cambridge University, 1993.

————. *Inevitable Revolutions: The United States in Central America*. New York: W. W. Norton, 1993.

————. *The Panama Canal: The Crisis in Historical Perspective*. New York: Oxford University Press, 1989.

Linn, Brian McAllister. *The Philippine War, 1899-1900*. Lawrence University Press of Kansas, 1999.

Minger, E. *William Howard Taft and American Foreign Policy*. Kent, Ohio: Kent State University Press, 1975.

Offner, John L. *An Unwanted War*. Chapel Hill: University of North Carolina Press, 1992.

Paterson, Thomas G., et al. *American Foreign Relations: A History*. 5th ed. Boston: Houghton Mifflin, 2000.

Pérez, Louis A., Jr. *The War of 1898*. Chapel Hill: University of North Carolina Press, 1998.

Schoultz, Lars. *Beneath the United States: A History of United States Policy Toward Latin America*. Cambridge: Harvard University Press, 1998.

Stanley, Peter. *A Nation in the Making: The Philippines and the UnitedStates, 1899-1921*. Cambridge: Harvard University Press, 1974.

Vázquez, Josefina, and Lorenzo Meyer. *The United States and Mexico*. Chicago: University of Chicago Press, 1985.

For Students

Abodaher, David J. *Puerto Rico: America's 51st State.* New York: Franklin Watts, 1993.

Bosco, Peter. *World War I.* New York: Facts on File, 1991.

Cooper, Michael L. *Hell Fighters: African American Soldiers in World War I.* New York: Lodestar, 1997.

Dolan, Edward F. *America in World War I.* Brookfield, CT: Millbrook Press, 1996.

———. *Panama and the United States: Their Canal, Their Stormy Years.* New York: Franklin Watts, 1990.

Frost, Mary Pierce, and Susan E. Keegan. *The Mexican Revolution.* San Diego: Lucent, 1996.

Gay, Kathlyn. *Spanish American War.* New York: Twenty-First Century Books, 1995.

———, and Martin Gay. *World War I.* New York: Twenty-First Century Books, 1995.

Granfield, Linda. *In Flanders Fields: The Story of the Poem by John McCrae.* New York: Doubleday, 1996.

Jantzen, Steven L. *Hooray for Peace, Hurrah for War: The United States During World War I.* New York: Facts on File, 1991.

Kent, Zachary. *World War I: "The War to End Wars."* Springfield, NJ: Enslow, 1994.

Leavell, J. Perry. *Woodrow Wilson.* New York: Chelsea House, 1987.

Markham, Lois. *Theodore Roosevelt.* New York: Chelsea House, 1984.

Randolph, Sallie G. *Woodrow Wilson: President.* New York: Walker, 1992.

St. George, Judith. *Panama Canal: Gateway to the World.* New York: Putnam, 1992.

Schneider, Dorothy, and Carl J. Schneider. *Into the Breach: American Women Overseas in World War I.* New York: Viking, 1991.

Stallings, Laurence. *The Doughboys: The Story of the AEF, 1917-1918*. New York: Harper and Row, 1963.

Stefoff, Rebecca. *Theodore Roosevelt: 26th President of the United States*. Ada, OK: Garrett Educational, 1988.

Stewart, Gail. *World War I*. San Diego: Lucent, 1991.

Takaki, Ronald. *Raising Cane: The World of Plantation Hawaii*. New York: Chelsea House, 1994.

INDEX

Page numbers for illustrations are in **boldface**.

JAMES LINCOLN COLLIER is the author of a number of books both for adults and for young people, including the social history *The Rise of Selfishness in America*. He is also noted for his biographies and historical studies in the field of jazz. Together with his brother, Christopher Collier, he has written a series of award-winning historical novels for children widely used in schools, including the Newbery Honor classic, *My Brother Sam Is Dead*. A graduate of Hamilton College, he lives with his wife in New York City.

CHRISTOPHER COLLIER grew up in Fairfield County, Connecticut and attended public schools there. He graduated from Clark University in Worcester, Massachusetts and earned M.A. and Ph.D. degrees at Columbia University in New York City. After service in the Army and teaching in secondary schools for several years, Mr. Collier began teaching college in 1961. He is now Professor of History at the University of Connecticut and Connecticut State Historian. Mr. Collier has published many scholarly and popular books and articles about Connecticut and American history. With his brother, James, he is the author of nine historical novels for young adults, the best known of which is *My Brother Sam Is Dead*. He lives with his wife Bonnie, a librarian, in Orange, Connecticut.